Critical Acclaim for the Writings of Bill Neel

"This is a must-read book. Bill takes you on his historical journey through Arkansas. His whimsical tales and recollections will make you laugh and even bring a tear to your eye."
—Willy the Clown

"Uncle Bill is the real deal, an actual treasure in my life. We enjoy our days together with our Arkansas adventures. I really like to see him writing and laughing while I relax on my green blanket. I love you, Uncle Bill!"
—Rocky B. Neel, PhD

"Meow! Meow! Meow. . . Meow. . . Meow, Meow, Meow, Meow!"

Rocky translates: "Amazing! Great! Uncle Bill's words are Simply Poetry. . . I highly recommend this bestseller to all cats—even lions!"
—Puff Neel

"It's a fun, off-the-wall read—a great book to take your mind off life's problems."
—Mhigh

Also by Bill Neel

Sooner or Later:
The Stories and Adventures of the Odd Triple

Cactus S. Neel and Puff Neel:
"Want to hear us sing?"

Cactus the Wonder Dog:
A New Leash on Life

Bill Neel

Lost Coast Press
Fort Bragg, California

Cactus the Wonder Dog:
A New Leash On Life
Copyright © 2023 by Bill Neel

All rights reserved. No portion of this book may be reproduced in whole or in part, by any means whatever, except for passages excerpted for purposes of review, without the prior written permission of the publisher or the author. For information, or to order additional copies, please contact:

Lost Coast Press
155 Cypress Street, Suite A
Fort Bragg CA 95437
cypresshouse.com   800-773-7782
Cover: "Want to go get a chocolate chip cookie?" and Frontispiece
© 2023 Bill Neel
Boston Terrier drawing: istock.com/JSatt83
Paw prints: istock.com/ Volodymyr Kotoshchuk
Book production by Cypress House

ISBN: 978-1-935448-46-4
Library of Congress Control Number: 2023935065

Printed in the USA

2 4 6 8 9 7 5 3 1

First edition

For Addison Nicole Neel

Table of Contents

Chapter One:	Cactus the Wonder Dog	1
Chapter Two:	My Mom's Passing in Altus, Oklahoma	19
Chapter Three:	How I Got to Know Rocky the Wonder Dog	25
Chapter Four:	What Makes Rocky So Special	39
Chapter Five:	Rocky the Wonder Dog with Too Much Time On Our Hands	43
Chapter Six:	Willy the Clown and the Shirley, Arkansas, Homecoming Parade	47
Chapter Seven:	Old-School and Babysitting a GPS	53

Cactus the Wonder Dog
A New Leash on Life

Cactus the Wonder Dog

Several years ago, I had a support-service dog, Rocky the Wonder Dog. Rocky was a Boston Terrier, and he was like my right arm. A couple of years ago I lost Rocky to a brief illness. I was in my eighties and didn't want to bond with another dog. A few months went by and this family in Little Rock had a Boston Terrier that was extra-hyper and they could not control him. His name was Chaos. (No such word in the dictionary). Chaos was about to walk his last mile. He is an older dog, and the family didn't have a lot of choices. A family in the area where I live, related to these folks, told them I had just lost a Boston Terrier support-service dog. They also called me and asked if I wanted to take this dog. I started to tell them no, I just couldn't do that right now. All of a sudden, this family struck a nerve: they said, "He is a Boston Terrier, an older dog."

I thought, *Well, I'm an older person, and maybe Chaos and I could grow older together, since I'm in my eighties.* That evening, they brought him into my home, and it was like he had always lived there. They told me to keep him inside as he might run away. Oh, was *that* wrong! As time went along he about caused *me* to run away.

I knew I had a gold mine, but it was getting the gold out of the mine that was a chore. After I had worked with him on his manners and other small problems, he was not the same dog. I no longer wanted to call him Chaos. Sometimes it's hard to pick out a name for something special. I thought about this awhile. I guess in a way he gave me an idea for his name. He came to me and looked at me like, "When do we have lunch?" I hadn't noticed that he was a beautiful dog with special markings. His other master had not noticed that on his forehead there is a marking of a cactus. He picked up the name very quickly. He has now had the name for over a couple of years. I think that was really his name to start with, but Uncle Bill was the only one who knew.

Bill Neel

Cactus really likes to ride. He doesn't care if it's around the block or a hundred miles. He went to the bank with me and found out that if he was nice, the young ladies would give him a treat and show him a lot of attention. I was also showing him a lot of attention, and this was just what he needed. One morning I had an early appointment at the VA in Conway, Arkansas. Like I said, Cactus loved to ride. He always stayed in the pickup unless I told him he could get out. I stopped in this small town in the middle of nowhere, and Cactus jumps out. I had stopped to get gas and watched him run off. I was about to go crazy, but the lady in the station came out and said she would tell people in the town about the pretty Boston Terrier running away. Gosh, I had only had him a couple weeks or so. I continued to pump my gasoline, and could not run off to look for Cactus. I had a doctor's appointment. I hated to leave him; I had worked hard with him, and never expected anything like this to happen. I decided to drive around hoping to find him. Like I said before, I had no time to waste. I drove around the area three times—and nothing. I told the lady at the station I had to get to my appointment, and would be back in a few hours. She said, "By then someone will probably find him."

Cactus The Wonder Dog

Cactus had a collar and a tag, but sometimes even all that doesn't help. I decided to make one more round of the area, and if nothing, I would just have to go. After still no sign of him, I stopped in front of the station and said a prayer: *If Cactus shows up now, I will be so happy.* Just as I was about to leave, I look in my outside mirror and here comes Cactus. He jumps in the truck as if to say, "Have you been waiting long?"

I have a leash for him when I let him out of the pickup. I was not using the leash the proper way. It took me awhile to learn how to use it. Boston Terriers are very smart dogs. It might take me a while, but Uncle Bill is smart too. You would think learning to use a leash would be something really simple. Just hook it on the collar and hold the other end and take him for a little walk. Keep reading the book and I will explain how to cure jumping jacks, or should I say jumping Cactus?

I was on a busy interstate highway and had to pull over for a minute. I got out of the pickup and Cactus almost jumped out. Oh, my little nerves! He would have looked like a pancake. Instead of *I hoped* it would be more like *I jumped.* At this time my poor nerves were really done in—worst case I had ever seen. I had to cure this, or I might wind up with jumping jacks too.

Bill Neel

I can usually catch on to things really quick and get things connected before they get this far out of hand. It was getting close to winter, and I went to a sawmill a few miles away to get some firewood. Now, this is a large sawmill with several employees. I had tried really hard for a long time to cure Cactus's jumping jacks. When I was in the army, we did jumping jacks early every morning. Cactus did them at all hours during the day. I had to get out of my pickup, as they didn't have curb service. Those giant saw blades were making so much noise you couldn't hear yourself think. Little did the employees know that Cactus was a part-time sawmill inspector. I tried to catch him before he went inside where the action was going on. In just a second or two all the employees ran out, screaming louder than the blades were screaming, saying a dog was in there near the blades and was going to come out sliced thinner than turkey bacon.

Since no one was there to bother him, Cactus had plenty time to inspect the sawmill. In a short while, he comes outside like he's saying, "What's all the excitement going on out here?"

Two guys grabbed him and put him in my pickup. They said, "Mister, don't bring this dog back. We don't want to see pieces of a dog on the floor."

Cactus The Wonder Dog

I did some serious thinking on the way home. I had been looking at what would solve my problem, but hadn't thought about it, since I was spending most of my time trying to keep Cactus in the pickup. It was the steering wheel. I would tie the hand-hold part of the leash to the open parts of the steering wheel. The leash was long enough so that as Cactus jumped out it would hold him in his tracks but he would not be injured in any way. I would sometimes leave the window down and he would jump out. Then he would have to stand there until I got back. He finally decided he didn't want to play jumping jacks any longer. He has more games in his head than an elephant. I was so glad I found the cure for jumping jacks that I took him to the sawmill again. They saw me coming and they looked worried. I opened the door and Cactus jumped out. He could only stand by my door. Everyone at the sawmill was so happy I'd come up with this idea before it was too late.

Now for the eyeglasses, chocolate chip cookie, and cattle-rustling episode. As you maybe can see, I have very little time for writing a book or doing my chores. Now you can understand why his former master named him Chaos. Many, yes, many times I have thought about going back to his previous name. Maybe someday, if they put "chaos" in the dictionary, I might have second thoughts. (Not really—Cactus will always be Cactus.)

Now for the eyeglasses. My nerves are somewhat better, but with this I might get temper tantrums. If I can handle all the things you just read about, this part is like a walk in the park. It might sound as if I were making this up. Only my hairdresser knows for sure. I will say Cactus really does all these things. At times I wish I was stretching the truth just a little. I have an end table next to my recliner. I always, yes always, put my glasses on it for safekeeping. I have done that for a while. This way I can walk to them, and there they are. Do you begin to get the picture? One day I reached for my glasses, and it looked as if they had taken a walk in the park. I looked everywhere, inside the house and all around the front and back of the house. No sign of my glasses. I just knew it wasn't Cactus. He was playing with a dog across the road. I was trying to blame the tooth fairy for taking my glasses instead of my tooth! I thought, *No, I quit believing in the tooth fairy yesterday.* I knew it had something to do with the boy. He and I are the only ones living here. Cactus finally came home. He had a guilty look on his face when I started rubbing my eyes and kept asking him about my glasses. After a little while he went outside to this tall grass and stood there. I looked in the grass and—this is no joke—there were my glasses! The frames looked like even the trash man wouldn't take them. The lenses were nearby and looked to be in good shape. I hadn't had those glasses very long. I decided to go to the Dollar Store and get some cheap glasses just for the frames. I took the lenses out and put my lenses in the frames and they lived happily ever after. Believe it or not.

Now for the large chocolate chip cookie. Cactus and I had to go to North Arkansas, almost to the Missouri line, to pick up some birds. He can't stand these birds, but he just turns the other cheek. We got our cargo and didn't stay around long. I was not familiar with the area and had no GPS or road map. That turned out to be Cactus's advantage. I managed to get on the wrong highway, and nothing in sight to get directions. After driving for a while I saw this beautiful building. They made homemade pastries and were packed with customers. I was dressed in old work clothes like I'd been rode hard and put away wet. The manager, a really nice young lady, asked if she could help me. I told her I was lost and told her where I needed to go. She said a lot of people got lost in this area and gave me the directions I needed.

Bill Neel

She asked me if I would like to try one of their famous chocolate chip cookies. It was as big as a pancake. I tried to pay her, and she said, "This one's on me."

I thanked her and started on my way. I got one small bite of the cookie and put it on the dash in front of the steering wheel where it would be safe. Seems I have used that phrase before. I was a little hungry but couldn't eat the cookie while I was driving. The pickup was getting low on gas, so I stopped to get some. Seems I remember another gasoline story in a small town in the middle of nowhere at night. I thought, *Uncle Bill, get that out of your head—what could possibly go wrong now?* Maybe I had forgotten about my big chocolate chip cookie in a safe place.

As I got back in the pickup, I looked on the floor, and the little sack my cookie was in—yes *was in*—was now empty, and Cactus had chocolate all over his face. He looked at me as if to say, "The Cookie Monster took it." They say chocolate is bad for dogs. Don't believe a word of that. This happened over a year ago and Cactus is still about the same. I am going to find a safe place to hide and see if he can find me.

Now for "Cattle Barking." Cactus rides with his feet in the seat and paws on the dash, looking for herds of cattle inside fenced areas. He seems to know when to start looking. The cattle can't hear him bark. A lot of times he goes wild and puts his feet on top of the seat and barks at them through the back window. I have found out that if I want to keep anything safe, put it in the back of the pickup, unless it is raining. If it's raining, don't go shopping. I started to keep quiet about this one, but I'm on a roll (or a chocolate chip cookie). I'm doing a lot better since my little nerves left me.

We shall call this episode "Who Ate the Sandwiches?" It wasn't the Cookie Monster. He was full. I have some nice neighbors across the way. They are always really busy and usually eat a sandwich for lunch. They had the makings of a sandwich on the seat of their pickup. They made a mistake by opening the door. Cactus was looking for a handout. He ate everything but the bread. He will never eat the last of anything. I haven't seen the neighbors in a while.

A few weeks later their son needed some help. We went to help them. They live at the bottom of a mountain, in a nice cabin that has a deck with a great view. They have a couple of uncovered rain barrels near the deck. Does this sound like trouble brewing? Cactus just loves water. He sees the barrels and jumps into one of them.

Bill Neel

He has a bog swimming pool across the road, and has no problem with the pool, but if we hadn't been there, he would've drowned in the rain barrel. Does this seem like a show that was on TV several years back? The neighbors' kid had some problems too.

Now, Cactus and his swimming pool, it begins to get a little better. All the things I have written about happened over a two-year period. Like Cactus loves water like a duck, and most always will jump in a pool if one is handy. He can get out of these pools with no problem, but there seems to be a small problem with his pool. He was going for a swim the other day and five of the neighbors' ducks were in his pool. Rather than cause a commotion, he had a talk with the ducks to get a better understanding (oh, yeah, he also speaks Duck.) After several hours of discussing the matter, Cactus told the ducks they could swim on Mondays, Wednesdays, and Fridays. He would swim on Tuesdays, Thursdays, and Saturdays. They could all jump in the pool on Sunday. We will see how this works out. Some days, if it's really hot, Cactus forgets what day it is.

Now for the last little episode. Cactus is like a little kid. I know better than to play this game. He gets really, really serious, and every time we play this it gets out of hand—

Cactus The Wonder Dog

especially the hand that is pulling his nose. I tell him a hen lives here, a pullet lives here, and a rooster lives here. Then I ask him, "What lives on your nose?" I don't give him time to answer as I pull his nose off and wiggle my thumb between two fingers. He gets really wild until I put his nose back on his face. It's a wonder I'm still here to write this. I don't play this game very often.

Now for a brighter side of our adventure. Cactus has a pretty girlfriend he's been seeing for several months. They go to the park for picnics and hours of fun playing keep-away. Cactus has a favorite stuffed toy he has played with forever before he met the love of his life at the park. Her name is Sally S. Hatter. It was love at first sight. Cactus saw Sally playing on the slide and quit playing with his stuffed toy. To break the ice he asked her about the weather. Now, this was the start of summer. I think it was easy to break the ice at that time. He told her his name was Cactus S. Neel. She said, "What a cute name. My name is Sally S. Hatter."

Cactus asked her about the "S" in her name. Sally said, My folks didn't have a baby book, and since my first name was Sally, another "S" couldn't hurt anything, so I was known as S. S. Hatter."

Bill Neel

Sally asked Cactus about the "S" in *his* name. He said, "Honey, I don't want to brag, but my master was reading a history book about the late President Harry S. Truman. He didn't have a middle name, and took the letter 'S.' Gosh, it's like three peas in a pod with us."

Sally began to cry about how smart Cactus and his family are. She said her master was a first-grade dropout with a lot of dollars and no cents. Cactus said, "Don't cry, Sally S. Boston Terriers are really, really smart. I have a lot of cents and no dollars. This will be the perfect marriage. The money situation will work out just right.

"Now, since we have that worked out, what about my stuffed toy? You are always taking him away from me and trying to hide him under the merry-go-round. I will admit it's really a good place to put important things. We could open a Merry Go Round Bank. We can put our money under there and it's hard to get it out. Pretty soon we would be millionaires."

Sally said, "When we get old the merry-go-round will have so much money our kids can crawl under it and spend it in one day. Sally begins to cry really bad. When she quits crying after a few hours, she says, "They're your kids too.

Cactus The Wonder Dog

Cactus says, "Just hold on a minute. As you might remember, you said your family didn't have any cents, just all dollars. I don't remember my family throwing many nickels and dimes under the merry-go-round."

Here Sally goes trying to cry again. She now has extra-dry eyes and has to get a couple of water buckets and throw water on the floor, hoping I will mop it up.

We don't eat very often. When she stops crying, I take her out to get a sandwich. We haven't even gotten engaged as of yet, and look at what has gone on. It's a wonder she didn't throw a fit when I brought a potted meat sandwich and cut it in two, trying to see that both of us had the same amount. I kept eating on her half, trying to even it up, and before long she didn't have anything at all. I felt bad about this, and I had thoughts of getting her a complete sandwich. Gosh, they are only a quarter. I reached in my pocket and I had no cents. Sally had all dollars. The people at the deli had no cents to change her dollar. They were rich too. A few choice words were spoken before I could get Sally S. out of the deli. As she walked on the sidewalk with me, her eyes were so dry she began to use some really choice words. Since she couldn't cry, the choice words were flying from her mouth. It was really cute that we had to walk home, which was several miles, because the car was out of gas. We didn't have enough cents to put gas in the car, since it was over seven dollars a gallon. I would have asked Sally for a dollar, but we are only going together. I've got more cents than that. We finally made it home and she opened a new sack of dog food (not the cheap kind she serves me). Well, she means well. I had already had a potted meat sandwich.

People ask me how I can take all this. I tell them, "If I can take all this before I tie the knot, I won't have to tie the knot after I get married, so to speak." A little while later I asked for Sally's paw in marriage. She got all mixed up: She thought I was asking for her dad. I said, "Honey, you know the English language—you can take almost any word and make all kinds of soundalike words that are spelled different. So much for all that highfalutin talk, Sally. Since I am a genius, you may have a little trouble understanding me in our marriage. Now what about our honeymoon? I'm not one to spend a lot of money, but I've got a lot of cents. There is a beautiful motel right next to our cheap apartment. We can put on our swim trunks and mingle with the people who are about to jump in the pool. Honey, I just love water."

Cactus The Wonder Dog

After staying there for a few hours, swimming and having dinner with our friends, we decided to take in a movie. Sally says, "Cactus you are so smart, no wonder you have a lot of cents."

Now, Sally has never heard of a drive-in theater. It's cheaper to go through the cotton fields and rice paddies. You know our boy Cactus—spend little and save a lot of dough. As they leave the pool to take a walk in the country, Cactus tells Sally she has to carry her own hip boots. He tells her he can just barely carry his own.

Honey says," Cactus, I love you so much I will carry one of your hip boots."

Cactus says," Honey, that is so sweet we will put it on page three of our marriage book."

Honey says, "That is so sweet. These hip boots are so heavy I just might have to drag yours until we get to the rice paddies. By then we should be able to see the screen."

Cactus tells her not to draw a lot of attention dragging his hip boot. "Drag it in the brush alongside the highway, so people going by won't see an extra leg. If they do stop, you can tell them you are frog hunting and that when you get the boot full you go home."

"You know something, Cactus, I really think people will believe it. Just what are we going to tell the people at the drive-in theater concession stand as we are sitting in the chairs with rice paddies and cotton all over us?"

"Sally, we will cross that field to the concession stand after we cross it."

"Cactus," she said, "you are one of a kind. I have gone to movies with gentleman callers and they take me to the theater and go inside. I have never walked through water, mud, and rice paddies wearing hip boots to save a dollar and a quarter per person, and above all, tonight is Get in Free Night. No wonder the people in the concession didn't say anything about our booties. Now we have to walk back home."

"Sally, why didn't you tell me it was Free Night?"

"Cactus, you know yourself I don't have any cents. Don't you remember when you tried to borrow a quarter to get a soda at the concession stand? Cactus, have you thought about getting a job? That way you would have more cents."

"Sally, the only job I have ever had was barking at the racecars as they sped around the track. They went by me so fast, by the time I started to bark they had already passed me twice. My boss said, as slow as I was I would still be barking an hour and a half after the race was over.

Cactus The Wonder Dog

"Now there were some great benefits for my barking. I could always spot my car on the parking lot when the race was over. I think being unemployed fits my personality. Let's try getting on a game show. It would be my luck to win a car or a train or maybe a plane. I would spend years of my life barking at the TV station to pay all the taxes. I think what I really need to do is wear my hip boots to the drive-in theater and wonder how I ever got into this story. Wearing them on Free Night would always be a blast. I think I could handle this while you keep a good steady job to keep us going."

CHAPTER TWO

My Mom's Passing in Altus, Oklahoma

The Strange Journey Back

I don't want to lose this thing that happened to me on the way home from Oklahoma. All of this is 100% true. I'll try to spell good too.

Annie Lee Neel Perry
9/22/1916–2/18/2009

Today, September 22, 2016, would have been Mom's one hundredth birthday. In the late 1990s, Mom moved to Cleburne County, Arkansas, and bought some land—five acres with many, many trees. Mom did not like all the trees on her land. She was raised in southwest Oklahoma where, at night, you could see a town thirty-five miles away. I like the trees.

Mom was the last of the family I grew up with. Delbert B. Neel (my dad), and Bobby K. Neel (my brother) had passed away. I visited Mom every chance I got. I called her every day. If she didn't answer the phone, I called the police to check on her.

As time passed, Mom's health got bad. Mom's doctor tried to get her to go live in a retirement home, but Mom would have nothing to do with the idea. That doctor tried everything. He finally sent a therapist to talk to Mom. He was out to prove that she was unable to stay in her apartment alone. Mom was always on the go, even at ninety-one. She would call a taxi to go shopping, and rode the church bus on Sundays. She knew the books of the Old Testament and the New Testament, and she knew the Hebrew alphabet. The therapist told the doctor, "She knows more than I do."

Mom went back to Altus, Oklahoma, but it wasn't too long before waning health put her into a retirement home. I moved into Mom's apartment, and went to the retirement home every day. I played games with her, and pushed her around in her wheelchair.

Bill Neel

Around 5 p.m. on February 18, 2009, Mom passed away. I had two weeks to move her belongings from the apartment before another month's rent was due, so I went to U-Haul and got the biggest enclosed trailer I could find. When the man at the U-Haul asked what model pickup I had, and I told him it was a 1995 six-cylinder Ford F-150, he suddenly seemed unsure about dealing with me. At that time my F-150 was fourteen years old. I try to take care of my things, and I've still got that truck. It's twenty-two years old now, and—oh, yes—it's got almost 300,000 miles on it!

I didn't know many people in Altus, and was unable to find anyone I could hire to help me with Mom's things. Well, years ago I worked for Ken-Mac Van Lines in Altus. I can handle most anything. I'm also an army veteran, and the Lord was helping me too, as you will see. I wasn't feeling very well since Mom had passed. I was seventy-one at the time. I might give out, but I never give up. I didn't try to rush. I had plenty of time to get everything done. I took a lot of breaks. Mom had a favorite chair, a La-Z-Boy recliner. I waited to load it last.

I had a little problem: There were a few things I couldn't get in the trailer; so I put them in the bed of my pickup and strapped everything down real good. Mom's recliner was one of the items in the back of the truck.

I like to drive at night and run with the big rigs. I left Altus and drove to Lawton, Oklahoma, then caught the H. E. Bailey Turnpike to Oklahoma City. I checked my load just before I got on I-40 to Fort Smith. Everything was fine. As I drove awhile on 1-40, I wondered if Mom's chair was still with me. I stopped a few times for coffee and to be sure everything was okay—big rigs push a lot of wind. Hey, I was seventy-one and acting like I was twenty! I was pretty beat when I got to Fort Smith. I checked the load there and it was still in good shape. I thought, *I'm not going to check it again until I get to Clinton, Arkansas.* I made it to Morrilton, then took Hwy. 9 to Clinton where I stopped for gas. The sun had been shining for a while, but I felt very, very beat. Remember what I said: "I might give out, but I never give up."

I was so happy to be almost home, but just as I pulled into the station, Mom's recliner came flying out of the pickup and landed in a ditch. It was not on the highway; and looked to be in good shape, so I thought, *It's not in the way. I'll get gas, take a break, then deal with it.* I took a long break, then backed up the pickup near the chair. When I got out of the truck, this young man said, "I'll get that into the truck for you." I didn't know this person, had never seen him before. I offered to pay him, and he said, "No, I'm glad to help."

I was so tired that I didn't know how I was going to get Mom's chair into the pickup, but with his help, I was able to load it. I started on my way, and turned to go to Shirley, Arkansas. I looked, and the young man was behind me. I thought, *He must live in the Shirley area.* I turned toward Fairfield Bay, and he turned too. When I passed Fairfield Bay, he was still behind me. After a few more miles I turned onto my road. He did too. I thought, *He must be a neighbor.* Curious now, I stopped my pickup and he stopped too. I walked up to him and he said, "We're going to help you unload your things. I've got my son on the way to help us."

Remember how I had to put the recliner in the back of the pickup, and it rode nearly 1,000 miles and didn't cause trouble until I got to Clinton, Arkansas? I'm sure Mom was looking down. The Lord and Mom knew how wearied I was. That man and his son were a huge help. I tried to pay them, but they wouldn't accept. I asked them their names, but they wouldn't tell me. It's been seven years since then. This being Mom's hundredth birthday, I wanted to write this today.

To this day, I still have Mom's chair in the barn. I will never forget what you guys did for me. I know the Lord blesses your families every day. I'm seventy-eight now, and still going strong. The VA offices in Little Rock and Conway have also helped me, and a lot of my friends have been there for me. I always help people when I can. I try to greet everyone with a smile and ask, "How are you?" My little dog, Rocky Neel, will not bite you. He minds his master. Thanks again! I'm so glad to be a Razorback. Go Hogs!

Bill Neel and Rocky

CHAPTER THREE

How I Got to Know Rocky the Wonder Dog

It was the middle of 2013. I was walking my three-mile trip to highway 16 and back to Bell-E-Akers. At first it was Fowl-Play-Akers, but the hawks took care of that. I started bellyachin' a lot about those birds speeding. Oh, well, it gave me another name for my ranch. This name seems to be right. It is now October 2016, and it's still Bell-E-Akers.

Now back to Rocky the wonder dog. My grandson had just left to seek his fortune. Also, his last going-away party. It would be okay if he got a job as a dish washer. He wouldn't have to look at all the dirty dishes.

Cactus The Wonder Dog

He had to leave Ace, his dog (Ace will also be in my book—it's a real sad story about Ace), and leave his cat too. A lot of people have said it was Ace who invited Rocky to visit him (so to speak). Ace would walk with me every morning. I didn't have him on a leash. We hardly ever saw a car until we arrived at the highway. I would never, never let Ace on the highway. Ace would visit everyone along the way. Ace was not a pointer, he was a smeller. Oh, the words I come up with. That nose was always close to the ground and running. One day Ace and I came home. It was like any other day. A few hours later, I noticed a cute little Boston Terrier in my yard. If this was true about Ace inviting (Jack) Rocky to Bell-E-Akers, I could understand. (Jack) Rocky's little legs were not able to keep up with us, and it took him a couple of hours to get here. He was really that small. You will notice (Jack) in several places in our story. You will see after a while that this was, I will say again, a real important word. (No, it has nothing to do with a beanstalk.) Now back to Rocky the Wonder Dog. I had never seen such a pretty little puppy. I didn't want to get attached to him—yes, it was a "him." I thought I had sung my last hymn when my grandson left. Ace had the three cats. I guess he couldn't speak cat too well, and now he had someone to communicate with. I just knew that any day, someone was going to claim him. I put flyers everywhere. I would show him to people. No one seemed to know anything about him. He didn't have a collar or tag or anyone claiming him.

"Oh, no—did he come from Roswell too?" (Ha-ha.)

In a short while, (Jack) Rocky started walking to the highway with Ace and me. He began to keep up with us pretty good. I would not let (Jack) Rocky on the highway. It's a wonder he listened to me. If you teach man or beast, the teacher has to be smarter than the student. Ace was doing a better job at this than I was. They both spoke the same language. Ace would still run with that nose close to the ground. We would be at the highway for a minute or two, and then go home.

As I put in parts of my book, I hardly ever get depressed. I'm so busy laughing I don't have the time. A short distance from the highway, there was a beautiful home. It had been there for a good while. I saw it built from the ground up. I knew for a fact, after I found out who lived there, that this home would feature my grandson and (Jack) Rocky before it was all over. I really enjoyed my walk to the highway every morning. All of a sudden, it was like two years had gone by. I didn't think

Cactus The Wonder Dog

about where Rocky had come from anymore. I had taken real good care of him. I took him to the vet. Regular. He had a collar and a tag. I got his teeth cleaned. He bonded with me more than any dog I had ever had in my life. Rocky came to me just when I needed him, and the way it looked, Rocky needed me. He had passed three homes on his way to my house. I found out later that he was not happy where he was living and was always running away. He would be going along the highway and people knew where he belonged and would bring him home. When he came to the bottom of the mountain, I had no clue where he was from. One day, as Ace, Rocky and I were about to go home from the highway, the man who lived in the beautiful home said he wanted to show us something he had. My friend Steve, who had some property farther down from me, was with us, and we all went over to check it out. Even Rocky the Wonder Dog. The man's home was a short distance from our turn-around spot. As we walked to his home, the man said, "Where did you get that Boston Terrier?"

I said, "He came to my house two years ago."

"That is my dog," he said.

I told him, "Well, you can have him back if you pay two years' groceries and vet bills." He looked like he'd been hit with a blivet. (We used that word in the army back in 1961 and for years after. Don't ask about the word, just accept it—or maybe Google it on your wristwatch). I would have never guessed where Rocky was from. Not only that, but as time went by I found out what Rocky's name had been before I changed it. My horror-scope says I can bide my time until things are better. One day I took Rocky to the vet. There was a man waiting in line ahead of us. He said, "That dog looks familiar. That's Jack." I don't know how many times I have taken him home."

I told him, "His name is now Rocky.

He said, "Come here, Rocky," and petted him. Then he said, "You've finally found a good home."

That was so touching. Will this story make a good movie? It's not over yet. I have a lot more to tell you. It was always exciting to watch Rocky and Ace with their noses to the ground, like four eyes are better than two. One day, as we were walking home, Rocky and Ace were big-game hunting, so to speak. They found out real quick that the little game gets real exciting too. When it was all over, Uncle Bill had to help them with a big stick. The brush was not real high in this large field, and Rocky and Ace thought they were the kings of the field, until they spotted two young—well, it wasn't Melon Collies (ha-ha). I can't find the right word, "Cayote," in the dictionary, so I will call them Melon Collies (ha-ha) and let it go at that. They were not hungry. They just wanted to play. If this had been their parents, it would have looked like a fast-food hotdog place. Well, it all started out as play and games, but then the coyotes began to get a little serious. Ace started to scream. He and Rocky were running faster than any horse ever in the Kentucky Derby. I found a large tree limb. Rocky and Ace ran right by me. When the coyotes saw me with the big stick, they decided to go find someone else to play with.

Did Rocky and Ace learn a lesson from this ordeal? Did Uncle Bill learn a lesson? I guess not. He got back into a bigger mess than that. I usually get a few days' break before Rocky and Ace stir up something. This was an ordinary day to start with. Little did I know it was going to end with fowl play. Never a dull moment. As we were walking to the highway, there was this culvert in the ditch to this house, so the people could drive over it and keep the water flowing in the ditch. Well, it hadn't rained in a good while, and someone had a family inside this culvert, and they didn't want to be disturbed. These are real mean critters when you get their feathers riled up. These birds are serious, except when it comes to Thanksgiving or Christmas. It's mostly their tame cousins you see on the table. I had never had a fight with a wild turkey before. This is all true, everything from the time Rocky first came to my house. I will let you know when I'm joking. These mother birds with babies will take on man or beast to protect their family. I was looking eye to eye at a mother turkey. When we were walking by, going to the highway, there was just a little warning. Rocky's and Ace's noses were always getting them in trouble, and as we came back from the highway, they just had to give the mother turkey some good advice.

It would have been better to keep walking. I don't think she needed any advice. She'd had plenty of time to think about the advice she'd got from us a few minutes earlier. We were not as clear on our game plan as she was on hers. Just before the culvert, Rocky and Ace thought they had it all planned out, but the mother turkey came rushing out like she was on fire. I guess that is the right word to use. She was pretty hot, all right. We are not talking about a ninety-pound weakling. As fast as they were going, Rocky and Ace didn't even have time to scream. They were so scared that they ran behind me like, "Uncle Bill, get your big stick."

I had never been so scared before either. I didn't think all this would get so much out of hand. The turkey ran at me like I was the matador at a bull-turkey fight. These birds don't act like this unless they have babies. She hit me on the leg on her first pass. I couldn't find anything to defend myself with. I couldn't take my eyes off this big bird. She was not fighting the ones who'd started all this mess. I could just see Rocky and Ace sitting back there in the stands, eating popcorn and cheering me on.

I was getting a raw deal. The matadors always have a sword; I didn't even have a pocket knife. She came at me again. I gave her a little kick as she went by, not enough to hurt her, but I let her know I was not taking any more. At this time, Rocky and Ace ran by, heading home. If a cop had been there, they would have gotten a ticket for speeding. All of this distracted the mother turkey and gave me a chance to be on my way. I wasn't running, but I was sure walking pretty fast. I knew she wouldn't get too far from her babies.

You think I'm finished talking about Rocky and Ace now, don't you?

Bill Neel

Oh, no!

This one is cute and funny.

A few years ago, I saw a movie about a small boy, his dog, and his mom and dad. The boy had to move several hundred miles to another state because his folks found better jobs there. The boy has a dog named Pete, and the two were bonded like Rocky and I are. The family were not able to take Pete right away, so they left him with a friend. It was really upsetting for both the boy and the dog. Dad told the boy they would be back to get Pete in a few weeks. The family didn't know, but Pete escaped from the friend's house soon after they'd left. The boy was always worried about Pete, and thought he was still with their friend, who was afraid to call and tell the boy Pete was gone.

A few weeks went by and the boy's dad told him they would go get Pete that weekend. One day before they were going to go, the dad was coming home from work and saw a long line of cars stopped on the exit he took to go home every day. He thought it was a bad accident, and got out of his car to see if he could help. As he walked down the road, he could see he was really the *only one* who could help, because Pete had taken the exit too, and was now blocking traffic. Somehow, Pete

Cactus The Wonder Dog

had made it to within a couple of miles of where his young master lived. Animals are smarter than people at times. The dad got Pete, put him in his car, and they finished Pete's journey home.

Now, you can see what happens if your dog or cat is bonded with you. When Dad came home with Pete, his son could not believe it. Pete had traveled hundreds of miles! I wrote this to show how strange things happen.

I have some friends who live a ways down from me. They have one dog and didn't need another. Someone had dropped off a Pomeranian. Most always, you have to buy those dogs. I guess this would soon be Uncle Bill's discount. They called me, and I tried to tell them I was already in the doghouse, so to speak. Crazy me, here I go again.

Ace would never ride, and I couldn't open the door to the pickup fast enough for Rocky. I looked at this little dog and I could already see the writing on the wall. Those little legs would be a major problem for him, as active as Rocky and Ace were. Someone had taken real good care of this dog. I would never find out very much about him, but his little legs didn't look as long as some of those gopher matches I have mentioned from time to time. If you have never seen any of them, they are pretty small. No, I did not name him Gopher. That's a cute name, all right, but I named him Pete after the faithful dog in the movie. Pete would walk a short distance from the house, but he never made it to the highway. Most of the time, I would carry him.

One night a big snowstorm came, but we didn't let anything stop us from our walks. I was trying to get out of the house and leave Pete where it was warm. Rocky and Ace were having a good time running and playing in the snow. As we got started on our walk, Pete was in the house screaming and crying—it was really loud for such a little dog. Like they say, "Dynamite comes in small packages." When I went back to get him, he got so happy and excited. I carried him to a spot to where he could walk a little in the snow just like the big boys. I turned my back for a minute, then turned around to check on him, and he had gotten into a snowbank. All you could see of him was his little nose, and not much of that. I grabbed him and took him back to the house. Rocky and Ace were still walking and playing.

I hated to do this. It really broke my heart. I had gotten attached to Pete and he had gotten attached to me, but I knew this wasn't the right home for him, and it wasn't right for me to raise him this way. I'd bit

Cactus The Wonder Dog

off more than I could chew. I would never drop off a dog or cat or any other type of animal in the middle of nowhere, so I called the animal shelter and told them what I had and that I couldn't raise him proper. They put Pete in a small cage and he started crying. I started crying too. I tried not to show it. Again, that was the hardest thing I've ever had to do. I knew he was in good hands, but I would never get to see him again. This was three years ago, and it still touches me. A few weeks went by and I went to the shelter and asked them about Pete. They said he didn't stay at the shelter very long. A man, a woman, and a little boy took him to a good home. I felt better about this. Remember the movie? Pete now belonged to a man, a woman, and a little boy. It is really something how things happen to me!

Bill Neel

I just can't quit bragging about Rocky. Every time we go to the VA he adds more people to his list of followers. As we were going to the pickup, there was this young couple trying to get a young German shepherd in with them; he was wild and looked like he'd had no training. Rocky walked on by like he didn't even see him. That put another feather in Rocky's cap. Sorry if I'm bragging too much, but as time goes by Rocky just seems to get better with all the things he was trained to do.

Bill Neel

What Makes Rocky So Special

I don't know how to start this. It's a true story, and I want to tell it to someone. This is extra-hard to do. I don't want these people to think badly of me for writing it. Like I've said many times, when I first came to Arkansas I had to start on the ground floor, but I'll try not to drag this out. I'm a softhearted person, and already a little tear has come to my eye.

Well, look at all the shows on TV. I said at one time that a person will complain he has no shoes but later sees someone with no feet. At times I get on the wrong road. Then I see what I have just written, and then I try to forget my small problems. It's hard not to think

Cactus The Wonder Dog

about your problems until you see a young man in a wheelchair, or a family that has just lost their home to a fire on Christmas day and lost everything they had. (All of the family survived. They could have lost family members.) I had a man with new shoes ask to trade his shoes for my old shoes. That's when I first came to Arkansas—Land of Opportunity. I don't see the young man in the wheelchair very often. He has a lot to be thankful for too. It could always be worse.

I want to tell you about what Rocky did. I'm very blessed that the Lord sent me this dog. He keeps me on the right track more than anyone will ever know. He can tell real fast when I am having problems. Seems he can tell when other people are having problems too. I walk with Rocky in several different areas: in Shirley, we walk by the ballpark; in Fairfield Bay, the walkway to Jack's Convenience Store; in Clinton, Arkansas, behind the Dollar Store, and in Little Rock, around the area of the VA. When I get to one of these places, I put a leash on Rocky and let him lead the way. When we are in our own area, he doesn't need a leash; he can just run and have a good time. He never gets out of my sight in case I might have some sort of trouble. A very smart dog.

Bill Neel

I listed those several places where I walk Rocky so that not one place will stand out as being where this happened. Rocky and I started walking. He took me to an area we hadn't visited in several months. Not a real popular place for us. I wondered about this at first, but I just go with Rocky. More people know Rocky than Uncle Bill. We sit on this bench—I mean, Uncle Bill sits on this bench, taking a little break before we finish our journey.

There were some people there, and you know how bashful Uncle Bill is. I didn't know these people, but I started talking to them. They were so friendly. Not often do you see this. As we talked, they told me that their home had burned to the ground last Christmas Day and they lost everything. That happened over three months ago. I hadn't heard anything about it. They were not asking for anything, and they had already built a new home. This really touched my heart. I've said this many times before: I try to help people all I can. Also I have said many times that you don't have to find me, I will find you.

I tried to write this such that I would not upset anyone.

Bill Neel and Rocky

PS: After a while Rocky was ready to walk again. He didn't want to go any farther, so he led me to the pickup to go home. It was like he had done his good deed for the day—again!

You don't have to find me. . . I will find you!

Rocky the Wonder Dog with Too Much Time On Our Hands

The other day, I told Rocky we were going on another outing. I said, "It will be several hours before we can leave. I told Rocky I had to get the clock on my cheap little phone fixed. No, it's not the battery—my battery has about as much spark as I do. I guess you could compare it with one of those gopher matches. You know, I haven't seen any of those in years and years. The reason they called them gopher matches was because of the old belief that you would strike one and then have to "gopher" a *real* match to get the job done. During that time, many, many people quit smoking. All the people trying to light up were smoking more than their cigarettes.

Now, back to the repair on my phone. It will cost me as much as $150 to get it fixed. I could get another phone with the $150 and have change left over. Rocky said, "Keep the phone you have." He said he'd never seen two cans with a piece of wire between them, and only about two feet apart. Most phones like that would have a sundial. You know, I got to thinking about the time I almost got married and gave my almost-bride all those lavish gifts. I think the phone would have tied the knot. We would always be real close together—even when we talked on the phone. When she fainted in the parking lot, I could have called her an ambulance. She would scream, "Call me an ambulance, call me an ambulance!"

I said, "Okay, you're an ambulance."

She hit me with the oven mitt I got for her. I'm sure glad I didn't get the cast-iron skillet. Rocky is getting more jealous by the minute listening to this. Well, I think I know why my phone is so messed up. It's not Rocky. I was always calling this lady who would give me the time, temperature, and a commercial. I had to call her a lot since I couldn't tell what time it was on my sundial at night. My quitting school in the middle of the first grade didn't help either.

The poor little phone was worked to death, and the lady was getting tired of talking to me, thinking I was flirting with her. Finally I told her I was going to get me a "grandfather clock." I could see the numbers okay during the day and use my gopher matches at night, and I would stop bothering her every couple of minutes. She said, "Why don't you get you a wristwatch like everyone else?" Then she gives me a big cussing out and says she is quitting her job giving the time and temp. She just couldn't take it any longer. It turns out I've still got the oven mitt my ex-bride threw at me. I just love happy endings.

Since I have the oven mitt I started (or almost started) my marriage with, would I say that I'm about to get married again? Who knows? I just know that Lucky Girl is out there somewhere. I already have the gift for my next bride.

Bill Neel

CHAPTER SIX

Willy the Clown and the Shirley, Arkansas, Homecoming Parade

I don't perform any longer—I stopped twenty years ago. I guess I could get a job with *The Old and Reckless Radio Show*. At that time, I didn't have Rocky, my support dog. He wants me to tell you folks he is as smart as two Border Collies. I told him it would be more like three, and he said, "No, just two." He didn't want to brag! With Rocky and me both bragging, I'll bet you've already left the parade. Maybe Shirley has, too. She'll find her way home.

Here I go again asking—and no matter how old I get I will keep asking—why, oh why, did they change the state logo from "Land of Opportunity?" It was like that when I crossed the state line the first time I came to Arkansas in 1968. If I had stayed in Altus, Oklahoma, I would have opened plumbing shops. My dad was a plumber. He had his license; but he liked his office in city hall much better. Now, back to my favorite topic: Land of Opportunity. There are many hundreds of people in the state of Arkansas who have proved this to be true. Some are gone, while others are there to keep their memories alive. It's like, my parents named me Billy R. Neel. I go by Bill Neel. I've had a lot of people tell me the names go good together. I named my support dog Rocky B. Neel. He goes to the VA in Little Rock with me when I have to go for checkups or anything else. Rocky goes into a lot of other businesses, but he has a big fan club in the VA. Strangers will stop us and say, "What a pretty dog."

I feed and take care of Rocky with the very best. He is with me 24/7. Now, let's not forget Puff; you can look at her and see that she does not want for anything—except for Rocky to get out of the way when I try to pet her. Can you see what I'm leading up to? No matter if I change my name to Joe or whatever; or if I change Rocky's name to Pepper; or if I change Puff's name to Baby Sally—oh, I almost forgot, if I change Willy the

Clown to Clipper the Clown). I have given out hundreds of my business cards with my picture on the front and my autograph on the back. Last price I had on Willy's market, they were worth 35¢ apiece. Pretty good, since they started out for free (ha-ha). No matter what you name anything—yes, anything—leave it like it is: "Land of Opportunity!" That way people will know it's the real thing (like a soft drink I know).

It's bad weather outside. I'm going to quit while I can see before the lights go out. I like to write. I never get stressed out doing this. You can speak to Rocky and me. We are there to show you that not everyone is stressed out and having a bad day. I was like that before I got Rocky. I am real blessed to have had him for several years. Not all dogs can handle his job, like not everyone can fly a plane. It takes a lot of training. You can check Rocky's record on how he performs in any of the places I have been with him. Oh, if you happen to notice, Rocky has the same color leash as his colors—black and white. For a long time I did not let people pet him. Almost everyone asked why. He is getting older, and I am giving him a few more things he can do. If he doesn't overdo it. You can tell when you see him that he is not the average everyday Boston Terrier. You can

Cactus The Wonder Dog

also tell Rocky and I are very much bonded and have been from the very first day. If you and your dog are not bonded, it's okay, but he or she can't do the work Rocky does. I know it's real hard for him at times. Rocky will never, never, never mess on any floors anywhere or anytime. I will say this is the way he really is, no matter wherever he may be. He will tell me when he has to go. There have been times he had held it longer than anyone would think possible. You too can be in Rocky's Fan Club.

The other day we were in the VA Hospital in Little Rock. It was almost time for the doctor to escort me to his area. Rocky had been there for a while. All of a sudden, he had to go. I told the lady at the desk I'd be right back. She told me it was ok. Rocky did his thing and we got back. They called my name. How about that for timing? Rocky rides the elevators and is real nice. He's been on every floor. I could write a short story about how I got him as a puppy. We won't bore you to death all at once. It's very, very interesting how Rocky's life started with me. We won't mention all the names and a lot of the details. Who knows—one of these days I can hand out two cards instead of one. I no longer entertain. These cards are old but they still look good.

We hope to see you soon. You can never tell where we may be. You can tell it's us for sure. Rocky has the only black-and-white leash we know of at this time (also a collar to match), and he is a very pretty Boston Terrier. We let a few people pet him now and then. Please ask first. Thank you.

Bill and Rocky Neel

PS: If I write about Rocky, I've got a lot more things to tell you about. Rocky says, "Hi!"

Old-School and Babysitting a GPS

I'm old, old-school, but I think you call it GPS—the thing that keeps you from getting lost. This involves Uncle Bill and Rocky the Wonder Dog. A few weeks ago, we were in northernmost Arkansas. I hadn't driven in the area for over twenty years. Anyone could tell Rocky had never been in these parts. Here is the way you can tell: if Rocky lies in his bed in the pickup, everything is okay. If he gets to an area he doesn't recognize, he's steady looking out the window, so in case I dump him, he will know his way back home. It's kinda like the little boy and girl and the old witch on that little weathervane that used to be real popular.

Cactus The Wonder Dog

Now to the GPS part. I told you I'm old-school. I don't use anything but RRT. That means "Rocky Road Telling." Rocky and I don't agree sometimes, and I have to give in when I don't see cars, road signs, or people. Rocky just sits there and bides his time until I finally turn around and go back where I started (and also need gasoline). You can see I don't give up easy. You'd think I would pay attention to RRT by now, but I'll never learn. What would I have to write about?

I was trying to get to this small town, and all I could see was curves for miles and miles. I finally saw a little mom-and-pop grocery, but no help there—it looked like it'd been closed since the days of the covered wagons, and they all went west to look for gold. I don't blame the highway department; they kept the road in good shape. I guess a few curves are good for everyone. I finally got on the right highway and there were still a lot of curves. Then I saw a sign that read this road is steep and has a lot of curves. Now, what would have happened if I had a GPS (just a little funny). It would have said, "Could you please stop your pickup truck? I feel dizzy and carsick, and I don't want to make a mess."

I will try to do the right thing for man or beast, so I let the GPS out. After a few minutes, I said, "Rocky and

I have a far piece to go, and we don't have time to sit here and babysit a machine."

It said, "Give me a little more time. Act like you're picking up aluminum cans; that way, nobody will think you're a nutcase."

I told Rocky to get in the pickup. I think he gave the GPS a short circuit. It said, "If you want to be that way, we can throw rocks at each other."

We saw a tractor coming with a great big mower. The GPS thought the mower was there to help it throw rocks. We got out of there pretty quick. That mower was not on anyone's side—it was throwing rocks at everyone. I'm sure someday, after recycling, it will be a GPS again.

Don't you just love happy endings?

Rocky and Uncle Bill